THE S.P.R.I.N.T MODEL

THE S.P.R.I.N.T MODEL is a unique system designed to improve overall performance results and reduce performance anxiety by strengthening an individual's emotional intelligence and critical thinking skills.

"BE READY AND WILLING TO GIVE UP EVERYTHING YOU ARE TODAY

FOR WHO YOU WILL BECOME TOMORROW"

BY: SHAUN SPENCER

THE S.P.R.I.N.T MODEL

THE S.P.R.I.N.T MODEL is a unique system designed to improve overall performance results and reduce performance anxiety by strengthening an individual's emotional intelligence and critical thinking skills.

BY: SHAUN SPENCER

What does S.P.R.I.N.T Mean?

Self-Awareness

This refers to having a deep understanding of yourself and your emotions. It involves being conscious of one's thoughts, feelings, and physical presence in the moment and understanding how these elements affect your performance.

Purpose-Driven

This means having a clear sense of your mission, values, and the significance of your creativity. It involves understanding the deeper reasons why you choose to be an athlete or performer, along with the impact you intend to have within your specific discipline.

Resilience

The ability to bounce back from disappointments, rejection, learning from failures, and learning to thrive, while maintaining your passion as an athlete or performer. Resilient athletes and performers not only have the ability to endure, but they are continuously refining their craft and using setbacks as stepping stones to perfect their performances.

Interpersonal Skills

Having interpersonal skills means having the capacity to interact peacefully and authentically with your peers, your audience, and your coaches/directors. These skills involve active listening, empathy, effective communication, and the ability to adapt to various personalities and situations.

Navigating Anxiety

This is the ability to recognize and effectively deal with the natural and often intense feelings that can occur before and during a competition or performance. It includes a combination of techniques, such as deep breathing, visualization, positive self-talk, and mindfulness. This allows you to use your anxiety and transform it into a source of heightened focus that will benefit you instead of hindering you. An example would be "Tunnel Vision".

Transformation

This represents the deliberate and systematic effort to enhance one's physical abilities, mental resilience, and artistic skills to reach higher levels of performance excellence. It embodies intense training, disciplined practices, and the cultivation of a growth mindset, with the goal of achieving personal milestones and surpassing limitations. Always evolving to be a top-tier athlete or performer.

LEGAL
DISCLAIMER

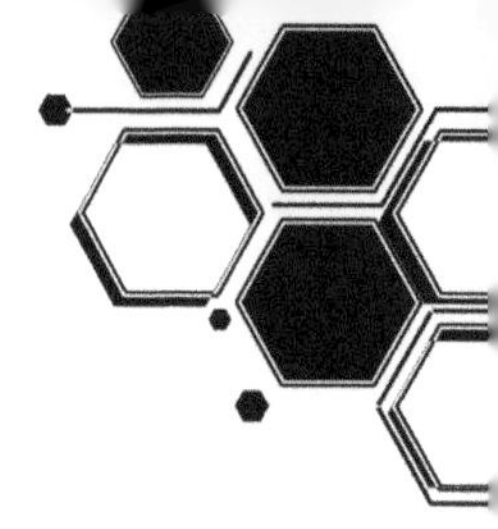

Shaun Spencer
Performance Mentor & Coach

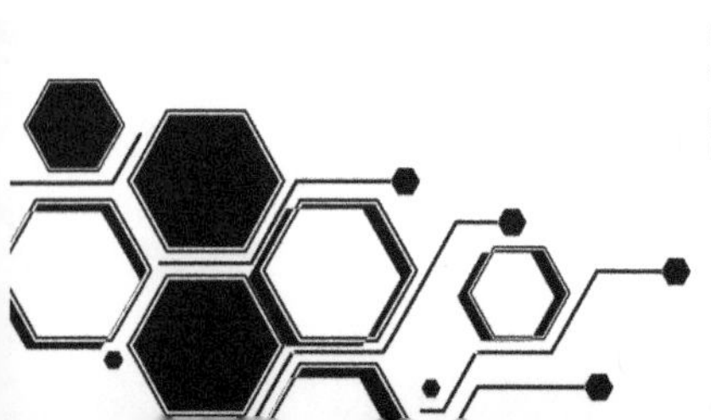

COPYRIGHT
INFORMATION

The S.P.R.I.N.T Model

Copyright © 2023 by Shaun Spencer

Printed in the United States of America
First Printing, 2023
ISBN 979-8-3507-0269-9 (Paperback)

For more information, contact
info@shaunjspencer.com
www.shaunjspencer.com

First Edition 10 9 8 7 6 5 4 3 2 1

Shaun Spencer
Performance Mentor & Coach

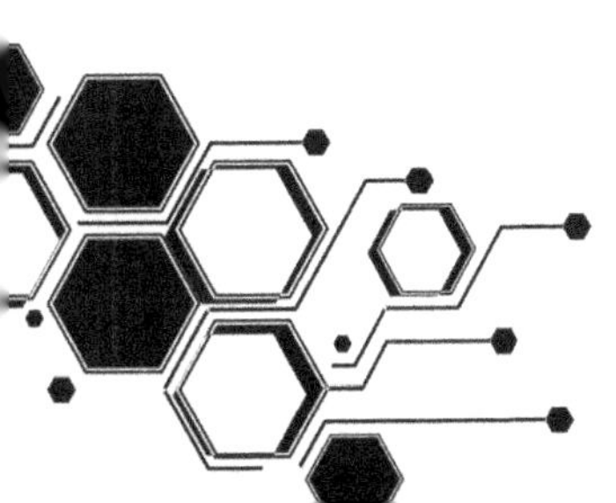

TABLE OF CONTENTS

What you will learn	01
What you can control	02
Meet Your Mentor	03
What is the S.P.R.I.N.T Model?	04
The Story of a champion	05
What are the benefits?	06
Self-Awareness	07
Purpose-Driven	10
Resilience	13
Interpersonal Skills	19
Navigating Anxiety	23
Transformation	29
Message from Shaun	32
Favorite Quote	33
Contact Me	36

THE S.P.R.I.N.T MODEL

What You Will Learn!

01. How to utilize emotional intelligence to enhance your performance results.

02. The different techniques I used to mange and overcome performance anxiety.

03. The different strategies I used as a professional athlete to improvo my training and competition results.

04. You will learn how to improve your leadership skills and communication skills as an athlete/performer.

05. You will learn meditation strategies and adversity training techniques that will assist you in improving your overall performance.

06. You will learn and acquire skills that will benefit you far beyond your career. Life skills that will serve you in other areas of your life.

What You Can NOT Control / What You Can Control

A large part of becoming an elite athlete or performer is knowing what you can and can not control in your life. Yes, this means choosing your battles wisely. Whether they are physical or mental.

CANNOT CONTROL 	CAN CONTROL 
The Weather	Preparing for different weather conditions.
Your Last Mistake	Whether you make that same mistake again.
The Future	How you prepare and show up for the future.
Your Competition	Studying your competition, learn his/her weakness, then adapt.
Stage Conditions	Practice performing on different stages in different environments.
Your Teammates	Being a leader for your teammates. Always being the example.

I'm Shaun Spencer

I'm Shaun, a Performance mentor located in Los Angeles. I'm a former professional Track & Field athlete, a Division II Championship Coach, and a college Hall-of-Famer at my university. My educational background includes degrees in Computer Information Systems Technology and Psychology with a focus on Human Behavior and Child Psychology. Beyond my athletic career, I've also been a professional runway model (New York Fashion Week), a part-time actor, a musician (3 instruments), and more. Yes, I did almost everything haha. So, I'm no stranger to the art of performing and the anxiety that comes with it.

Within my athletic career, I have been blessed to have been a professional athlete and have competed with, and beat some of the best in the world. Having said that, I am WELL aware of the mental and physical challenges that come with being an athlete or performer.

Just like you, I was and still am susceptible to the jitters that come when it's time to step into the spotlight and show the world what you're made of. But I'm happy to say that through my many years of competing and facing these mental challenges, I have learned a few key techniques to help improve performance results while combatting performance anxiety.

Welcome to
THE S.P.R.I.N.T MODEL

What is the S.P.R.I.N.T Model?

The Sprint Model is a creative system designed specifically to improve the overall performance of an athlete/performing arts specialist (Singer, dancer, actor, musician, etc.). It does so by building and strengthening the emotional intelligence of the individual, thus providing them with the tools to produce better results. In the past, we performers tend to rely solely on our physical talents, while neglecting the nurturing of our mental process. We do this, forgetting that, in order to become an elite performer (whatever our discipline is), we must nurture our minds just as much as we nurture our bodies. I dare say more.

In my younger years, I didn't understand how to utilize Emotional Intelligence as an athlete. For me, it was all about being faster and stronger than my competition. Yes, I was intelligent, but I only used it to outsmart my opponent. That's all. The thrill of competition is what gave me energy. If my opponent was bigger than me, I would use my speed against him. If my opponent was smaller than me, I would use my speed along with outmuscling him. If we were equal in size, I would study his moves, find a weak spot, and then use that to overcome him. So I guess I did use a little bit of Emotional Intelligence but it was more unconsciously then willing.

Once I began training as a professional athlete and started coaching, I began to develop a better understanding of why emotional intelligence was so important to an individual's performance. After learning this, it became the foundation of my training and coaching because it always produced results and led me to becoming a Division II Championship coach.

"The Story of a Champion"

A good example of using emotional intelligence is when I won the CIAA Division II Championships as a coach. We were a small and young team that had to compete against the top two teams in the conference that were made up of 50% or more athletes who had competed in Olympic Trails or had qualified to do so. So, from the beginning, trying to out-muscle them was not an option.

The day before the competition, we put together a plan to beat these giants. We decided that, instead of trying to beat them one by one, we would use a different strategy and simply outscore them. We understood that muscle and speed are not going to do it. We also remembered that college championships are determined by points, not by who gets first place. It was an "Ah-haaaaaaaa" moment. With that said, if we couldn't win first place, we wouldn't get mad. What we would do is take everything below 1st place. We would put as many athletes as we could in every event. This way, they can have 1st place (10 points), and after that, we would focus on taking the remainder places. This means that we would take 2nd (8 points), 3rd (6 points), 4th (5 points), and so on. So after every event, we would outscore the current champs every time.

Ultimately, when the day was over, they had more 1st place trophies, but we won the Championship because we had more points. This was the first Track & Field Championship ever won in the school's history.

So yes, being physically strong or fast is one thing, but being mentally strong and strategic is another. This is how you use emotional intelligence to overcome your challenges in your careers and lives.

Benefits of the Sprint Model

- ☑ **Reduced Stress and Anxiety (Nervousness)**: This will assist people reduce the nervousness that comes with competing, as well as handling the stress that comes with competing in front of others.

- ☑ **Improving Decision-Making Skills**: Our success depends completely on the decisions we make. This book helps performers make better strategic decisions before and during competition, such as making on-the-spot adjustments without panicking.

- ☑ **Improved Focus and Concentration**: This will help increase an athlete's/performer's ability to focus solely on the task at hand or what's most important. I call it, "Locking in on your target".

- ☑ **Performance Adaptability**: This increases the ability to easily adapt (adjust) to any changes in conditions within their environment. Things such as weather, competition, crowd size, and other things that can't be controlled. In other words "Being a Chameleon".

- ☑ **Building Resilience (Ability to recover from disappointments)**: This will strengthen the ability to bounce back more effectively and strategically from setbacks or disappointments, such as injuries losses, or bad performances.

- ☑ **Enhanced Performance**: This allows the athlete/performer to remain focused, calm, and confident, leading to improved performance while under pressure. A huge game-changer.

- ☑ **Positive Mental Health**: This book will help improve your mental well-being by reducing the risk of mental burnout, anxiety attacks, and even high levels of stress that come from competing.

Self-Awareness

Having self-awareness or being self-aware is all about understanding who you are as an individual, your strengths, weaknesses, and being able to control your emotions. This is being aware of who you are as a competitor (physically and emotionally). This heightened sense of self-awareness (knowing who you are as a person) empowers you to make better-informed decisions, set realistic goals (achievable goals), and optimize your performance. Here are a few proven exercises that will help improve your self-awareness.

1. **Self-Reflection (Daily thoughts)**: Journaling (writing) about how you feel (or felt that day) and the things that were great and not so great. Yes, this may sound boring, but I promise that you will soon learn how valuable this will be in the near future. You can sometimes see things better when you write it down.

2. **Strengths and Weaknesses**: In other words, having a clear understanding of what you are good at and what you need to improve on. Make time each day to write down these down. This will help you locate the areas that you need to improve on the most. Again, writing things down is always a great way to understand how you feel about things. Be honest with yourself and don't feel ashamed. We all have areas that we can improve on.

3. **Meditation (Your quiet time)**: This is about having some quiet time so that you can think, reflect, and mentally relax. This means No TV, no music, no friends, no family. Just you and your thoughts. Some of the things that I like to do is go for a long walk, the beach, a drive, or even a long hike.

GUEST
HOME
PERIOD

PURPOSE-DRIVEN

To be purpose-driven is to have a clear and meaningful reason or purpose for what you do in life. For example, why you are participating in a specific sport or performing arts. This is the thing that is beyond the competition and that makes you crave becoming a champion. Every professional in their careers has identified this. You must too.

Being a purpose-driven individual also shows that you are motivated by personal growth and a desire to make your mark in the world. Once you have identified this, it becomes another tool that will give you a competitive edge over your competition.

Here are two easy things that you can build to begin discovering and nurturing your purpose.

1. **Vision Boards:** Vision boards are a great way to create a visual representation of how you see yourself in the future. This will help you increase your mental focus and allows you to visualize and physically see who you aspire to be in the end.

2. **Personal Code of Ethics:** VERY CRITICAL. As athletes/performers, creating and refining your OWN personal mission statement or code of ethics, is key and will give you a mental edge over the competition. This will be the code that you live by day to day and that embodies who you are as a person, your goals, and your aspirations. This is your Creed as an athlete or performer.

Resilience

Resilience is 100% mental. This is the ability to endure (withstand) lifes challenges both mentally and physically, while also having the ability to recover faster, stronger, and wiser. This helps you recover faster from disappointments and injuries, giving you a competitive edge over your competition. As athletes and performers, we all know the world is full of different setbacks that can affect us. With that said, here are some proven exercises that can help build your resilience and make you a stronger person.

1. **Adversity Simulations (Training)**: Get involved with or create activities that challenge you mentally by forcing you to encounter different challenges. Then come up with solutions for recovery and success. Expose yourself to controlled situations so that you can build your mental toughness (resilience). I call this "Putting your mind to the test".

2. **Mindfulness Meditation**: This will help you stay focused, reduce stress and anxiety, and enhance your ability to handle pressure. This involves practicing breathing exercises during high-stress moments, and accepting how you feel in the moment without judgment.

3. **Goal Setting and Reflection**: This is the process of setting short-term and long-term goals. Breaking down your larger goal into smaller more manageable (doable) steps. Always remember to celebrate the small wins and not just the big wins. After each win, whether it's large or small, take time to reflect on those wins and the lessons learned from any setbacks that happened.

MINDFUL MEDITATION

Here is a great way to start practicing your Mindfulness Meditation. Remember that nothing is set in stone (permanent) and this is all about your success. So that means you can tweak (make changes) this and tailor this exercise in a manner that serves you best. Enjoy!

1. Find a quiet and comfortable space to sit or lie down.

2. Close your eyes and bring your attention to your breathing. Take a few deep breaths to help center yourself. Remember to inhale deeply and exhale slowly. Doing so will help relax your mind and your body.

3. Start to focus your attention on different parts of your body, beginning with your toes and slowly moving up to the top of your head. The purpose is to help you remove any other thoughts that are not serving you at the moment and help you focus on your mental relaxation.

4. As you focus on each body part, notice any sensations without judgment. If your mind wanders, gently bring it back to the present moment.

5. Continue this process for 5 – 10 minutes, gradually extending the time as you become more comfortable with the practice.

ADVERSITY TRAINING EXERCISE

Adversity training is designed to expose you to challenging situations, that help develop resilience and adaptability. Here are a few exercises that have produced great results and that you can do on your own.

1. **Simulate Competition with Distractions:** Set up a training scenario(situation) that is similar to your competition environment. Then introduce some distractions such as unexpected changes in conditions, maneuvering (moving) around obstacles, and even simulating distracting noises. Practice keeping your focus while performing in these different situations. This will improve your performance by at least 30%.

2. **Equipment Malfunction Drills:** Having the ability to think fast and adapt at the last minute, is a skill that will take you very far in your career.

 - Purposefully create scenarios (situations) in which your equipment stops working. From there, practice how you would recover and find a way to still get the job done. Get in the mindset of being able to do this and staying calm and relaxed at the same time.

3. **On-the-clock Decision-making:** This involves preparing tasks and events that have tight time constraints (time limits). Practice making quick and effective decisions while under the pressure of the clock. This will teach you how to make critical decisions under less-than-optimal (less than desired) circumstances.

ADVERSITY TRAINING EXERCISE

4. **Unpredictable Training Environments:** This is what separates the men from the boys, or the women from the little girls. Practice in different environments with unpredictable elements, such as changing weather conditions, uncomfortable surfaces or stages, and visually distracting environments.

Learn how to adapt your training routine to different settings and locations. This will help you enhance your ability to adapt to unexpected changes and challenges when they occur. This is a VERY useful tool for those who participate in outdoor sports or activities that involve variable conditions.

5. **Partner Challenges:** Challenging yourself is one thing, but having a partner who can help create different challenges for you is a huge advantage. Find a friend or family member who can practice with you and can give you some unexpected challenges to figure out. This can be unexpected movements, changing the rules or conditions unexpectedly, or even using verbal distractions (yelling and trying to break your concentration). This will help you a lot when it is time to perform and your competition environment changes.

Interpersonal Skills

This is about developing the skills to understand and effectively interact with the people in your environment. This will also give you the ability to mentally adapt to any environment. This is an important and incredible skill. This is what I call, "Becoming a Hybrid". As a hybrid, you can mentally adapt and blend into any situation or environment that is outside of your normal environment. This is something that I developed at a very young age but still had to learn how to control my thoughts.

After learning how to adapt, I learned how to take advantage of my environment and take out what I needed to be successful. But remember this. When it comes to adapting to an environment or situation, you must remember to remain the person you are inside. Always remember your Creed (your motto or the rules you live by) and not allowing your situation to change who you are.

Example 1 – A track athlete arrives on competition day and it's raining. He/she still has to perform but the rain is mentally and physically challenging. **Tip** – Accept that it's raining and there's no changing that. Warm up and test how your body feels with mock runs, jumps, or throws. Then take the information you have, and make your mental adjustments. Repeat the same warm-up with the new changes and see how you feel.

Example 2 – It is time for you as an actor to perform on stage and you learn that there are celebrities in the crowd. You get nervous and your hands begin to sweat and shake. **Tip** – Take 10 deep breaths and exhale slowly each time. Think about a place that makes you happy. Remember that you have trained hard for this moment and that these celebrities came to see YOU. See yourself as a superstar and they are your fans. Now Rock-Out!!

Tips to Improve your Interpersonal Skills

Here are a few tips on how to improve your **Interpersonal Skills** that have changed people around the world.

1. **Study Communication Techniques:** As a leader, one of the best skills to have is being a great communicator. Take an hour or of each day to study the top communication experts in the world. You can find them on YouTube and of course Google. Study what they do and how they do it. Learn what makes them the best at communication. Study what they say and how they say it. This is very valuable and will make you one of the best in the world.

2. **Study Conflict Resolution (Resolving Conflicts):** Study conflict resolution. Learn different ways to stop and also to resolve conflicts. One thing to always remember... the most important thing to another person is their point of view (how they see things). Instead of trying to be right all the time and ignore their position, let them know that you understand their opinion and that you respect it. This will help de-escalate (calm down) almost 90% of situations before they get too bad. This can help you and the other person come to an agreement that you are both happy with.

3. **Team-Building Skills:** Practice working with people who are different than you. Each person has a different way of doing things. It is always great to work with people who are different so that you can learn something different. Especially people who are from different cultures than yours. Each culture teaches something different, so learning from different cultures will be a huge advantage to have as a performer. Always be open to learning something new and different.

Navigating Anxiety

Anxiety of any type SUCKS!! This happens to sprinters who are waiting to start their race, or to actors who are preparing to get on stage in front of 20,000 people. Performance anxiety is something that happens to almost everyone who competes or performs on stage. But what is **Performance Anxiety**? By definition, it's the feeling of mild or extreme nervousness when it comes to performing in front of people. Or what is popularly known as **Stage Fright**. This can happen before and even during a competition or performance.

Research shows that over 300 million people have experienced performance anxiety or other types of anxiety. So yes, many people experience some form of anxiety throughout their life and it is completely normal. I can say for myself, I have suffered from 3 different types of Anxiety in the past. Performance Anxiety, General Anxiety Disorder, and even Panic Attacks. Yes, even I suffered from it in the past.

However, I refused to continue to suffer and decided to teach myself how to manage it and overcome it. This didn't happen overnight, but with time and continued practice, I was able to learn how to manage my anxiety and eventually learn how to control it. Now that does not mean that I do not feel extreme nervousness at times. I absolutely do. But I practice the different exercises that I have learned over the years and that helps me feel better.

I have added a few great exercises that help me reduce and beat my anxiety when it arrives. I am sure they can help you as well.

TIPS TO REDUCE / OVERCOME ANXIETY

After years of experiencing performance anxiety, I have learned different techniques to control and overcome it. Always remember to allow yourself to feel how you feel in the moment. If you are nervous, understand that it is ok and normal to feel that way. Research shows, over 300 million people experience some form of anxiety. So never be ashamed. Here are some fun exercises that will help you manage and overcome your performance anxiety.

Tip #1 - **Mental Practice:** Practice creating exercises that could activate your anxiety. Some great examples would be talking in front of a large group of people, Speaking to your family, and even talking with strangers in public. It may be a little uncomfortable at first, but with time it will become easy.

Tip #2 - **The Counting Method:** Learning to control your breathing and heart rate is extremely important when combatting anxiety. Most of the times, when experiencing anxiety, your heart rate increases and you start breathing fast. By doing a 3-second inhale and a 3-second exhale (8 to 10 times), you can slowly calm down your heart rate and breathing. With time, you can increase the seconds to 4 seconds, 5 seconds, and even longer. This changed my life.

Tip #3 - **Verbal Confirmation:** This is reminding yourself that what you are experiencing is 100% normal And that you are ok. Verbally communicating or "Talking" to yourself is a great way to calm yourself down. Who better to do it than you? Remind yourself that you are ok and that you are just very nervous. Tell yourself that you have worked hard and that you are ready for this moment.

"When Anxiety Takes Control"

I once trained a college triple jumper with a lot of potential to be the best in his division. We trained hard throughout the year and he would achieve a new personal best in almost every track meet.

We arrive at the CIAA Indoor Championships. Our goal was always to continue improving and put out a jump that could qualify him for the Indoor Track & Field Nationals. This was one of those days when you feel everything is going to be perfect and you feel at your best. I knew this was his day to qualify.

Jason's first 3 jumps were around 50 feet each, which was already a personal best. But to qualify for Nationals, he needed to jump at least 52 feet. We reviewed his first 3 jumps and decided what he needed to change for his last jump. Jason steps onto the runway, and the room gets quiet. He takes a few deep breaths, leans back, dips his head, and takes off running. You could hear a pin drop. He gets to the first board and jumps...... His first phase is flawless.....His second phase is flawless.... going into his third phase is also flawless.....But, while in mid-air, I see his eyes start moving around as if something happened. Jason's concentration is broken and he brings his feet down early, landing on his feet. This is what we call, "Running it out" instead of landing.

Everyone goes crazy and wonders why he did not finish his jump. I was even shocked because we would jump over 30 times in practice. This should have been another day at the office for him. With my hands on my head, I began walking around in circles and trying to figure out what happened. But then I remembered seeing his eyes move. I realized that I was right about what happened at that moment. Jason got nervous in the middle of his jump and did not know how to recover from it. I literally saw it in his eyes.......

Jason couldn't explain what happened and was very much speechless.

I walk up to him and, instead of asking him what happened, I ask him how he is feeling. I wanted to know how he felt about his jump. He then explained to me that he felt amazing and as if he was walking on air. He said everything felt perfect until something told him to look down and see how far he was into the pit. All jumpers know that you NEVER look down. Also, that while in mid-air, he began to question himself. He said he flinched (blinked) and brought his feet down.

I gave him a pat on the shoulder and told him that he did a great job today. I then asked him if he wanted to know something about that jump. He tells me yes. I say, "Well Jason, you may not know it, and it may haunt you for a long time, but when you brought your feet down, it was at exactly 51 feet". He starts smiling and saying "Noooo way". I say, "Yes Jason. Had you kept your feet up longer, you would have landed around the 54 feet. Which is a qualifying jump". He just smiled and said, "I almost had it. I know I can qualify now". I agree and we walk off to prepare for the next event.

Jason had second-guessed himself out of nervousness (anxiety) mid-jump and did not know how to recover from it. I only told him about the distance that he could have achieved because I taught my athletes to be resilient and to take everything as a learning lesson for the next competition. In life, being resilient and learning to control your mind is very important to your success.

  Shaun Spence

Transformation

This is the process of mentally transforming yourself to become the best you can be. **An Athlete's View:** If you are an athlete, it's learning about your competition, visualizing your competition the day before it happens, and then seeing yourself in the winner's circle.

A Performer's View: If you are a performer such as a singer, dancer, actor, or musician, it's visualizing your performance before you arrive that day. Visualize yourself on stage and see yourself perform better than you ever had thought was possible. Ultimately receiving a standing ovation from the crowd.

Tip 1 - **Goal-Setting:** This is about having a strategy for our short-term goals and long-term goals. Yes, having long-term goals is great, but it is the short-term goals that make the long-term ones possible. An example of a short-term goal would be winning your school's singing competition, while a long-term goal would be performing on "The Voice".

Tip 2 - **Tracking Progress:** Tracking your progress on paper (Or computer) and having regular review sessions with your coach will help see how well you are doing. Always have the mind for keeping track of how far you have come and overall progress.

Tip 3 - **Celebrating Milestones (achievements):** Remember that "A win is a win". Regardless if it is a large one or a small one. Celebrate any and all achievements to have to do with your personal goal. Again, the large ones are great but the small ones are where it counts.

MESSAGE FROM SHAUN

I hope that you were able to find a lot of value in this book and that you will begin to nurture your minds as much as you nurture your talents. It took me years to understand how important nurturing the mind is to the overall success of my career. It wasn't until I started competing as a professional and training for the Olympics, that I truly understood the benefits of strengthening my emotional intelligence.

We are all performers of some sort. Whether you are a Volleyball player or you are a Broadway singer, it all falls under being a performer. We just have different stages, courts, and fields. As an athlete, I was faster than most people my height and could jump higher as well. But I soon learned that I would become a far better athlete if I took the time to build and strengthen my mind.

Continue being great at what you do and always be a student to the game. Always seek to perfect your craft and learn from the professionals who are the best in your field. Study hard, eat healthy, get plenty of sleep, and never give up.

A QUOTE THAT CHANGED MY LIFE AND THAT CAN CHANGE YOURS.

> "Be ready and willing to give up everything you are today, for who you will become tomorrow."

This is a quote that I live by to this day and that has shaped my life for the better in more ways than I could have imagined. A lot of the time, our biggest battle or competition is within us. We become stuck in our comfort zones because of the fear of the unknown. We all know the phrase, "If you want to achieve things you have never achieved, you have to do things you have never done". Of course, this is said in many different ways, but you get it. The point is that in order to achieve that higher level of success, we will have to step into uncharted waters and yes, they will likely be uncomfortable at first.

But I promise, that is where the victory is. That is where you find who you are as an individual and what you are truly capable of. Do not attach yourself to who you were in the past or even who you are today. Be ready and willing to become who and what you need to be successful. That is the challenge I set before.

Godspeed my friends.

SHAUN SPENCER

PERFORMANCE MENTOR & COACH

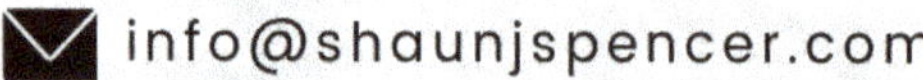 info@shaunjspencer.com

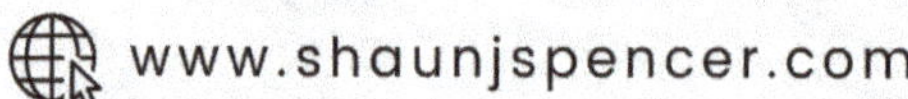 www.shaunjspencer.com

@IAMSHAUNSPENCER

@IAMSHAUNSPENCER

@IAMSHAUNSPENCER

Lets Stay Connected

Interested or Need Coaching? Let's Chat!

INFO@SHAUNJSPENCER.COM

MENTAL NOTES

MENTAL NOTES